DEALING WITH ILLNESS

STEPH GIEDD

childsworld.com

The Child's World
childsworld.com

Published by The Child's World®
800-599-READ • www.childsworld.com

Photography Credits
Photographs ©: iStockphoto, cover, 1, 5, 8, 14 (thought bubbles), 17; People Images/iStockphoto, 6–7, 22; Dean Mitchell/iStockphoto, 11; Antonio Diaz/iStockphoto, 13; Victor Brave/iStockphoto, 14 (kid in bed); Shane Kato/iStockphoto, 18; Art Marie/iStockphoto, 20

ISBN Information
9781503885370 (Reinforced Library Binding)
9781503885608 (Portable Document Format)
9781503886247 (Online Multi-user eBook)
9781503886889 (Electronic Publication)

LCCN 2023937457

Printed in the United States of America

BRINGING THE WORLD TO YOUNG READERS 1968

Steph Giedd is a former high school English teacher who now works as an editor. Originally from southern Iowa, Giedd lives in Minneapolis, Minnesota, with her husband, daughter, and pets.

TABLE OF CONTENTS

CHAPTER 1

When Illness Happens

Sometimes people become sick. They may feel ill for a day or two and then get better. But sometimes, people are sick for weeks, months, or even years. People may need lots of care to get better. Some illnesses are **terminal**. Others may have long-term effects. For example, some illnesses may cause people to lose their sight or hearing. They may not be able to move the same way they used to.

Getting sick is a normal part of life for kids and adults.

When people are sick, they might miss activities such as school or seeing their friends.

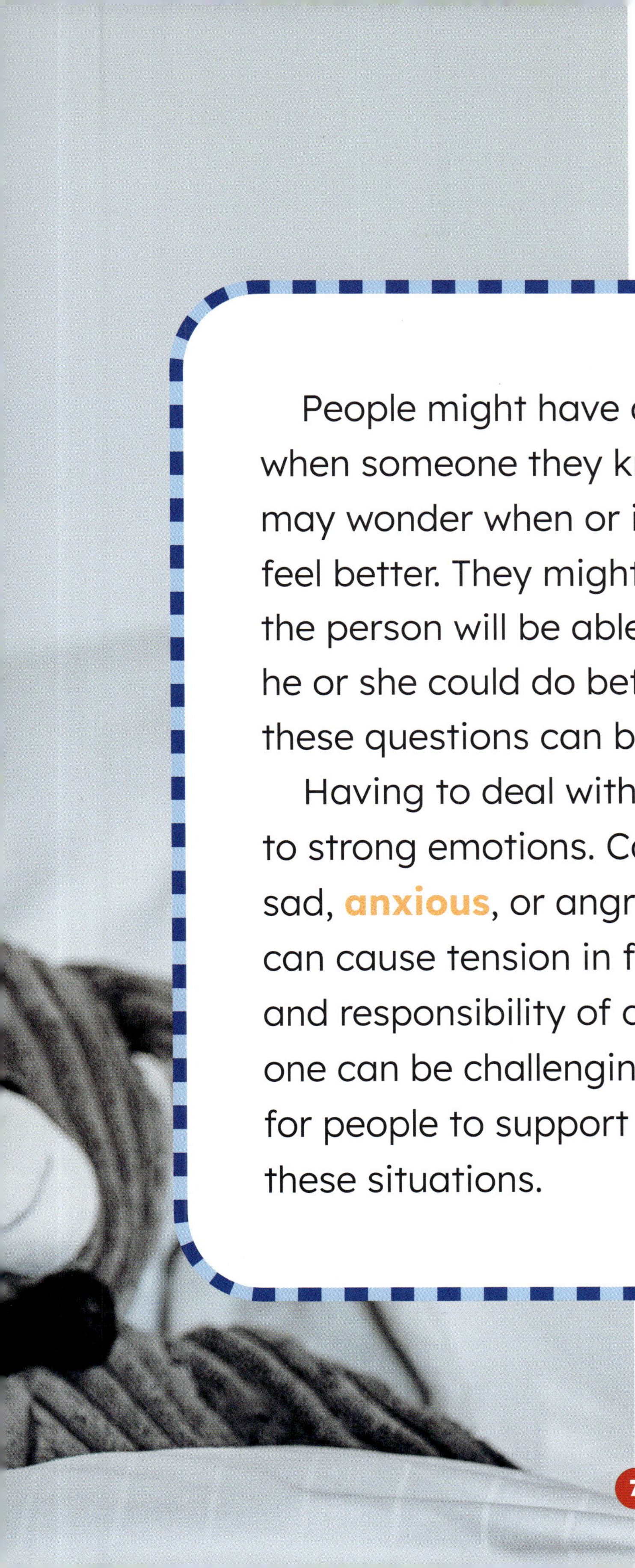

People might have a lot of questions when someone they know is sick. People may wonder when or if the sick person will feel better. They might question whether the person will be able to do the things he or she could do before. The answers to these questions can be scary.

Having to deal with illness may lead to strong emotions. Caretakers may feel sad, **anxious**, or angry. These emotions can cause tension in families. The stress and responsibility of caring for a loved one can be challenging. It's important for people to support each other through these situations.

Costly Care

Treating an illness like cancer can cost a lot of money. It might take years of care to get rid of the illness. Families may need to save money to pay for that care. This may mean skipping a family vacation. Or kids might have to wear the same shoes for another school year instead of getting new ones. People may need help from their friends and families to buy the things they need.

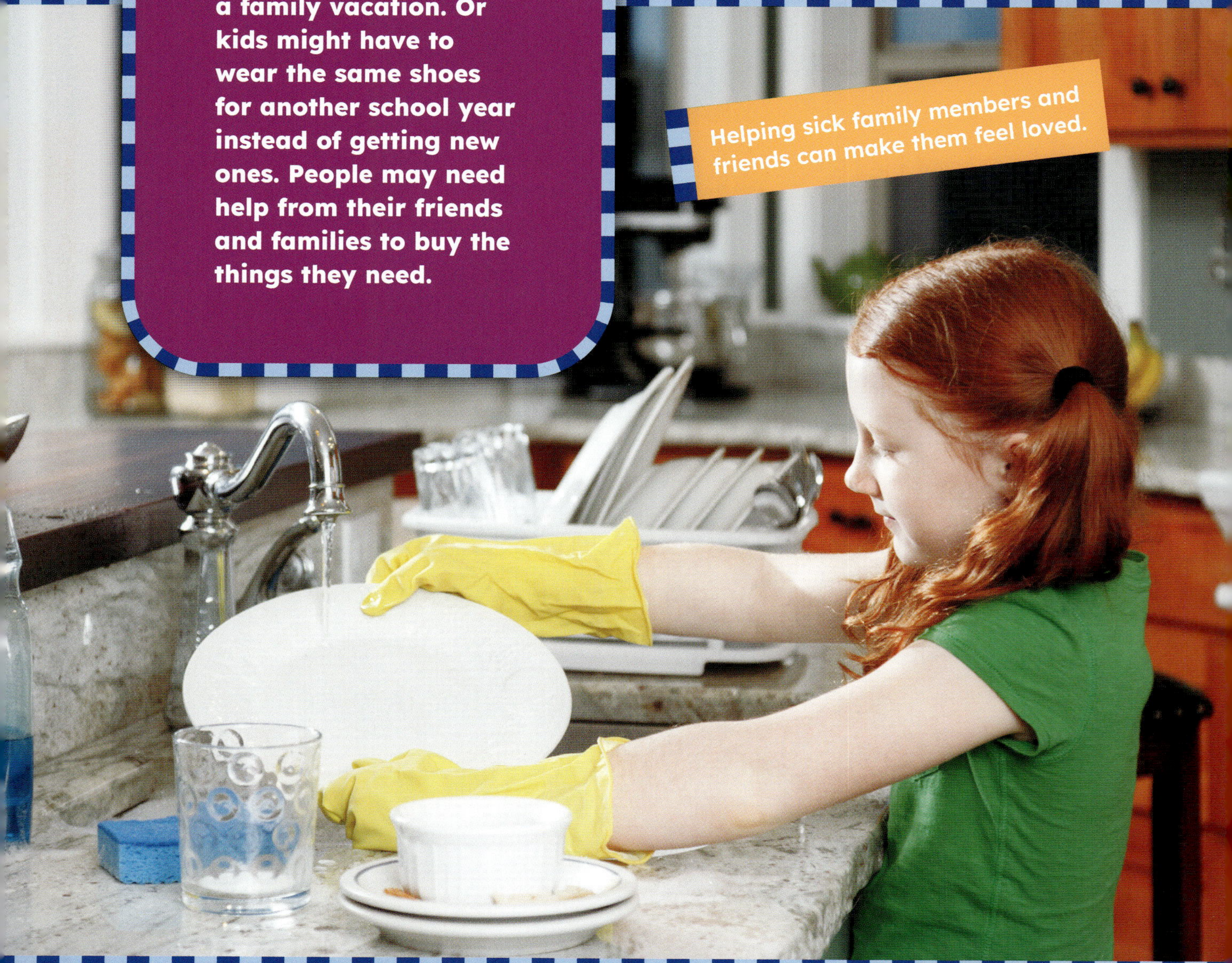

Helping sick family members and friends can make them feel loved.

Sick people may feel strong emotions, too. They may feel sad that they are sick. They might be scared about what will happen. Sometimes they may feel like they are a **burden**. It can be hard to care for a sick person. People who are sick may understand that. This may make them feel bad for their caretakers.

When someone is sick, family members may need to help more with household chores. They may also need to help care for the person who is sick. When a family member or friend becomes sick, the most important thing someone can do is to be there for the person in need.

CHAPTER 2

Coping with Illness

It is hard to **cope** with illness. But there are things people can do to make dealing with it easier. First, it is important to accept what has happened. This makes it easier to move forward and help the ill person. Accepting the illness can be difficult, even if the person who is sick will get better. It can be tough to go through an illness or see a family member get sick. Sometimes it seems easier to avoid it or ignore it. But that doesn't help anyone.

Hand washing can prevent people from getting sick.

When people are sick, it's important for them to take care of themselves. Illnesses like a cold, the flu, or an **infection** can make a person feel bad for days or even weeks. To feel better, it's important to get plenty of rest. Drinking a lot of fluids such as water, low-sugar sports drinks, juice, and warm soups helps the body heal faster. Some people may need medicine, but it's important to ask a parent or doctor first. Until the person feels better, it's important to stay home. It may be boring, but it will help keep others from getting sick. Staying home to rest will also help the sick person get better.

Some illnesses can be spread through sneezing, coughing, or touching.

It is important to ask how the sick person is feeling emotionally. Being sick can be lonely and scary for those who are ill. They may not know what is happening to their bodies. Not feeling well can be frustrating. Caretakers should try to have conversations with a sick family member to check in. The caretaker may not understand how the sick person feels. That is OK. It is important to listen anyway.

Being Sick Makes Me Feel . . .

When someone is sick, it is normal to feel a lot of different emotions.

Even people who are not sick might have strong emotions. It can be hard to see a loved one struggling with an illness. People can work through strong emotions by talking to family members or friends, seeing a **counselor**, or writing in a journal. Dealing with these emotions properly can help people feel less unhappy or worried.

When people are taking care of a sick person, they may forget to take care of themselves. But caretakers need to take care of their own health, too. They should make sure to eat good meals. They also need to do things they enjoy. Being active and getting enough sleep are ways people can take care of themselves.

CHAPTER 3

Helping a Friend Deal with Illness

Sometimes a friend may be sick. Other times, a friend may have a sick family member. Either way, the friend might feel sad or anxious about the illness. Friends need to support each other during these hard times.

When a person is sick, his or her friends can visit and bring a card or some food. They could also ask if their friend needs anything, such as a new book to read or an activity to do. All these actions can help lift the sick person's spirits.

Some illnesses are easy to see. Other times, people might look healthy but still be sick.

Phone calls and letters are good ways to keep in touch with someone who is too sick to visit in person.

Friends can also encourage the person to share his or her feelings. If the sick person does not know how to start talking about the situation, friends can ask questions. Some questions could include: Is there anything you want to talk about? What are you thinking about? How can I help?

Friends who are dealing with illness will have a lot of feelings. They may want to talk about their emotions. This might help them feel better. They might want advice. It might be hard to know what to say. That is OK. Sometimes just listening to a friend is the most important part.

It is OK if people dealing with illness do not want to talk. They might be tired of talking about it. Maybe they just need a hug. Or maybe they want to do something fun to take their minds off the illness. Other times, they may just want to know that someone cares.

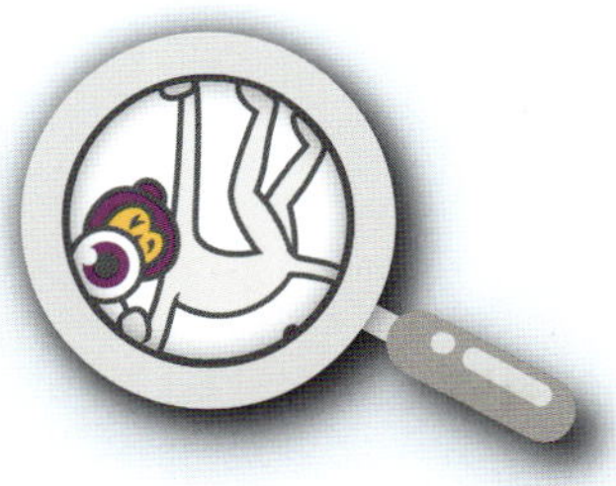

Wonder More

Wondering about New Information

How much did you know about dealing with illness before reading this book? What new information did you learn? Write down three new facts that this book taught you. Was the new information surprising? Why or why not?

Wondering How It Matters

What is one way that illness has impacted your life? If you cannot think of a personal connection, imagine a way the topic might affect other kids. What impact might it have on their lives?

Wondering Why

Why do you think it's important to learn about how to deal with illness? How might learning about this topic help you?

Ways to Keep Wondering

Dealing with illness can be a complex topic. After reading this book, what questions do you have about it? What can you do to learn more about how to deal with illness?

Fast Facts

- Illnesses can make people sick for short or long periods of time.
- Sicknesses can make people feel a lot of different emotions.
- Illness can cause a lot of stress both for the ill person and the ill person's loved ones.
- To handle stress, people can journal, be active, or do something fun.
- Talking to a parent, friend, or counselor can help people cope with their emotions.
- It's important for caretakers to take care of themselves.
- The most important thing to do for friends dealing with illness is to be there and listen to their feelings.
- Asking questions can help friends start talking if they do not know what to say.

Glossary

anxious (ANGK-shuhs) Anxious means to feel worried or nervous about something uncertain. People may feel anxious when their loved one is sick.

burden (BUR-dun) A burden is something that is hard to deal with. People who are ill may feel like they are a burden to their families.

cancer (KAN-sur) Cancer is a disease where the body's cells grow quickly and attack healthy parts of the body. A person who has cancer needs a lot of care in order to get better.

cope (KOPE) To cope means to deal with a challenge. People can cope with illness by talking to a counselor or writing in a journal.

counselor (KOWN-suh-lur) A counselor is a person who helps people work through strong feelings. When people are stressed, they can talk to a counselor.

infection (in-FEK-shun) An infection occurs when germs get into a person's body. When someone steps on a rusty nail, they may get an infection.

terminal (TUR-muh-nul) When something is terminal, it cannot be cured and will likely cause death. If someone has a terminal illness, it is likely the person will die.

Find Out More

In the Library

Bell, Samantha S. *Dealing with Loss.* Parker, CO: The Child's World, 2024.

Gaines, Arlen Grad. *I Have a Question about Cancer: Clear Answers for All Kids, Including Children with Autism Spectrum Disorder or Other Special Needs.* Philadelphia, PA: Jessica Kingsley Publishers, 2019.

Levine, Sara. *Germs Up Close.* Minneapolis, MN: Millbrook Press, 2021.

On the Web

Visit our website for links about dealing with illness:
childsworld.com/links

Note to Parents, Caregivers, Teachers, and Librarians: We routinely verify our Web links to make sure they are safe and active sites. So encourage your readers to check them out!

Index